香港國際詩歌之夜 *2011*
INTERNATIONAL POETRY NIGHTS IN HONG KONG

W0038478

編輯 Editors
方梓勳 Gilbert C. F. Fong
陳嘉恩 Shelby K. Y. Chan
柯夏智 Lucas Klein
何潔賢 Amy Ho Kit Yin
北島 Bei Dao

羅智成
Lo Chih Cheng

目錄 Contents

93霾雨：致永不消逝的「最後讀者」

這一次的春雨
開啟了兩萬年後達於全盛的冰河期
但沒人注意到。
只有我和兩天後
在潮濕的露店讀到這首詩的讀者甲例外。
我們擔心這個城市還來不及
揮霍它文明的巔峰
就已陷進深睡不醒的雪季
而整個亞熱帶的風景與垃圾
將成為下一個文明的石油與煤礦……
而在下一個文明之前很早很早的
這天下午
我和還沒有讀到這首詩的讀者甲
為躲雨走進這家以蕭索的人文精神著稱的酒館
腋下夾着來不及撐開的傘和一份
永遠擔心經濟不景氣的報紙
神情一如
淋得濕透的旗幟。

旗幟興風是為了作浪
為了撐起一片視野，被吹折也在所不惜
濕透的旗幟則整面糾黏在一起
像窩藏了一個標誌
或思想
或惡意
混跡於這個介於二十世紀末期和十九世紀末期

2

或上個冰河期與下個冰河期之間的
險惡環境裏。
我們，我和讀者甲，我們彼此之間的疏離
在於
我們並不曉得我們始終並肩列席
並在枯澀的眼底蘊藏着對彼此的期待
兩天後讀者甲在潮濕的露店
讀到這首詩，並短暫
被其中的訊息吸引
但他一直不知道作者甲曾和他相遇
在文明的每個險惡的時辰裏……

The Great Rains of '93
— To the Eternal "Last Reader"

This year's spring rains
are the beginning of an ice age that will blossom in
    20,000 years
but nobody has noticed.
Reader A, reading this poem
two days from now in a damp open-air stall, and I the only
    exceptions.
We are concerned that this city, before even
reaching the peak of its civilization
will get stuck in the snowy season of deep, unending
    sleep
and that all scenery and garbage of the subtropics
will become the next civilization's oilfields and coal
    mines...and long, long before the
next civilization
on this afternoon
I and Reader A, who has not yet read this poem,
find shelter from the rain in a bar known for its bleak
    humanist spirit
carrying under our arms an umbrella we haven't managed
    to open and a
newspaper always worrying about recession
with an expression on our faces just like
a flag drenched through and through.

Flags billow to make waves
and in support of a vision will not balk at being blown
    loose
but soaked flags clump together
seemingly harboring some sign
or thought
or scheme
conning its way into this evil environment
lying between the late twentieth and late nineteenth
    centuries
or between the last ice age and the next.
As for us the distance between me and Reader A
results from not knowing that we've been shoulder to
    shoulder
as non-voting delegates
with out weary eyes concealing a mutual expectation
In two days, Reader A in the open-air stall will
read this poem and briefly
feel attracted to its message
never realizing that he and Author A have met
at civilization's each and every evil hour...

(Translated by Lloyd Haft)

恐龍

我在博物館看到這隻恐龍
當落日灑滿軒窗，
寬敞的殿上，特大號的祭司
護守地球孩提的奧秘。

時間最大的標點
在失去的上下文中懸置……
遺落了果實的竹簍
這石與肉鑄成的雕塑
這搖晃的燈架，我感到
對肉體有着不可磨滅底
眷戀。

螻蟻列隊走過
巨大的腳趾虛懸
那曾是雷神的印戳
雨後遍蓋於
地球軟軟的額頭——
高聳的背脊
現在是斷裂的弓
無法蓄存一點力氣
空虛的頭顱
鬆脫了森嚴、綠色的歷史
弧度優美的頸項，
是修長的狹橋
連接飛鳥的視野

和龐大，憂愁
必然腐朽的軀體。

成排的肋骨
徒然的槳
在平滑如水的地面
船首翹起
顯然是重重地
撞在礁石上
當風輕拂
這繁雜的樂器輕響
一時沼澤復活
迷漫羊齒與薄荷的清香

我孤獨佇立。
在千窗環伺的大廳
憊倦的思維
才剛餵養了幻想的巨象：

那時岩漿還在卵石中流動
他們誕生在巨尾犁過的路旁
信賴地球，一如我們
活躍、貪吃，大致說來
也十分頑強。
現在他們成為沈默的矽礦
不再有樸素的慾念

和彈性的皮囊。
見證他們的星星都已太老
只有碳十四訴説着
千篇一律的臆想。

我在博物館
在一個偏遠的車站
看到這隻恐龍，
像拭過琥珀
我悚然而立。
它也曾有生命的條理
果肉包裹着果核
血液像清泉般
在裏頭川流不息
肥大的臟器在磨坊蠕動
養分從這兒傳到四處⋯⋯

我在博物館看到這隻恐龍
他們是神早期的作品
粗大，簡陋
但總是深情流露⋯⋯

Dinosaur

I saw this dinosaur in the museum
When the window panes were full of late sunlight—
an outsize priest in a spacious shrine
keeping vigil over the globe's childhood mystery.

Time's greatest punctuation mark
Suspended in the middle of a lost context...
A wicker basket with the fruit gone,
This sculpted amalgam of rock and flesh,
This teetering lamp stand. I sense its
Indelible attachment to flesh
and blood.

Armies of maggots march past
its gigantic foot is suspended in air
That once, after the rain,
Stamped footprints of the Thunder God
on the soft brow of the earth—
and the up-curved back
is now a broken bow
that can't hold an ounce of strength.

The empty skull
Has let go of its impenetrable green history
and the neck's graceful arch
is a slender bridge

joining the vision of a bird in flight
with a huge sad carcass
destined for decomposition.

Ribs in rows
Useless oars
on land level and smooth as water;
the prow jutting up
must have run up hard against
a reef
When strummed by the breeze
this intricate instrument resounds
and for a moment the swamp comes back to life
In a vague, vast scent of fern and mint

I stand alone.
In a hall with windows on all sides
my worn-out thinking
has gone to feed an imaginary mammoth

When magma was still moving through the pebbles
They were born beside the road
That a tail had ploughed—
Dependent on the globe, like us
active, hungry, and overall
indomitable.

Now they've become mute silica
No longer simple in their desires
Or pliant in in their skin.
The stars that witnessed them are too old:
Nothing left but carbon 14 to tell
The standard objective story.

In the museum,
At an out-of-the-way station,
I saw this dinosaur
looking like it was rubbed with amber
and I stiffened with awe.
The veins of life once ran through him
of pulp surrounding the fruit's core
and blood like a clear stream
flowing inside, an endless river.
Ponderous guts lurching in their millhouse
nourishment sent out in all directions...

I saw this dinosaur in the museum.
One of God's early works. Bulky, crude
But moving to behold.

(Translated by Lloyd Haft)

From CHINESE PEN (Taiwan), Autumn 2000

寶寶之書

5
復活是每天的：

我的思維被一隻濯足的蚊蚋
激起了漣漪
在薄如蟬翼的夢境
載沉載浮的我
被沖上黑暗之岸緣
攀附着被惦記的事
今晨
我再度醒來。

6
那箱每天都得重新打包的
日記，街名，失眠與考試卷的
從前
在來的路上我遺失了。

我每天都得重新編寫它們。

7
我允許你對我扯謊
至少再一千次
──誰會在你誠實的眼底仍希求
　　迂腐的真相呢？

26

我們是真正擁有過星星的
不像那些耽於幻想的人
我們在它下弦的地方
有個巨大的停車場
甚至我們還擁有
失去它之後的
憂傷

48

我率領大群星星奔馳
她說：「你為甚麼這麼興奮？」
我無法回答
我的神思正放着一萬個風箏

我花費半個夜晚到達那個隕石坑
但有人先我而至
在彼專心練唱

from Letters to My Darling

5
Revival happens daily

by a sandfly washing its feet, my thinking
is stirred into ripples
in a dreamscape thin as cicada's wings
now sinking now floating
I am washed up on the shores of darkness
Clinging to matters of great concern
This morning
I awaken yet again

6
That suitcase that needs to be repacked, every day, of
diaries, street names, insomnia, and exams
at some time in the past
lost on the way

I need to write them anew every day

7
I will allow you to lie to me
 at least another thousand to times.
—who would ever crave pedantic truths
from your sincere eyes?

26

We who have truly possessed the stars
Are not like the ones indulging in fantasy
Where it wanes down to its last quarter
We have an immense parking lot
And even sadness
Of all that was lost
Is ours to possess

48

I lead a cavalcade of stars
She asks: Why are you so excited?
I have no way to answer
My thoughts are flying ten thousand kites

I spend half a night reaching the meteor crater
But someone got there before me
Fully absorbed in his voice exercises

(Translated by Maghiel van Crevel, Nancy C. Ing, and Denis Mair)

蒹葭

一
在黑夜中
握着我的手的
你的手
是唯一的路了
你的手
忽弛忽緊
我也感覺到你
內心的坎坷

二
經過外露的河床、蘆葦
潮濕的礦脈
蜘蛛網,
網上的殘骸
鹿的茸角,和睡去而仍然
緊張着的聽覺
風,
翻開我們心頭的書
又合起

三
風
冷冷地向我們取明的燭火瞥了一眼
那乍暗而未復明的一瞬
妳華麗的愛情
驚惶地向我探詢
「聽，」
我說
風吹奏着羣山⋯⋯

四
一顆
印着貝殼的燧石
落下
一顆
印着星際航具的星
落下
一顆
雨滴
落下
我們抬頭
從萬千星星之中
去找這滴雨水的主人。

Rushes

1

In the darkness of night
Your hand
Holding my hand
Is the only road
Your hand
Loosening and tightening
I also sense the turmoil
in your troubled heart

2

Passing the exposed river bed and the rushes
Damp vein of ore
Spider webs,
Carapaces on the threads
velvet on deer antlers
and a sense of hearing asleep
yet still intent
Wind,
Turning the leaves of my heart
Then closing

3

Wind
Coldly glanced at the light of our candle
In that sudden moment of darkness
Your splendid love
Questions me in agitation
Listen,
I say
Wind playing the mountains like an instrument...

4

A piece
of shell-embedded stone
Falls
A star
imprinted with a spacecraft
Falls
A drop
of rain
Falls
We lift up our heads
among thousands millions of stars
to find the raindrop's owner

(Translated by Nancy C. Ing)

夢中書店

我們最敬畏、最著迷的叢林
正是那家書店。

在沒落社區一個
屢被郵差錯過的門牌裏
幾百里長的各式書架以及
石舖、鑲木以及
泥濘的甬道
壅塞、盤據
把知識延伸到
店裏一些還沒接上電力的地方：
布滿蛛網、迷瘴、
老鼠與蠹蟲的廳房、下水道、
水深及膝的地毯和
永遠失落了鑰匙的密室……

而高達數十層的書架、架上的巨型標本
殘破的旗幟、族徽、
封死的軒窗、失憶的抽屜
便一窟又一窟地向我們展示
人類心智猙獰的原貌……

沒有人，包括第三代店員八十九歲的ㄌ先生，
沒有人知道書店的實際規模——
包括去年為了追捕一本風漬書而
永遠沉淪於文字流沙中的文學教授、

多年以後突然從壁畫中破牆逃回的書評家
以及緊咬着他後領的新品種蝙蝠……
真的，即使緊守着乙區東側的書庫——
以傳記文學和寓言為主的灌木叢——
我們偶爾也會碰上一些
迷途者的骸骨……

我們最着迷的迷宮
就是那家書店了！
在變動不安的整整一個世代
我們幾乎是含着淚傳頌
那座不移動、不融化也不現形的冰山
而閱讀
讀那些冷僻、艱深的心靈——
以及持續不懈的幻想
就是我們青澀的教派每天的儀式……

像隻深藏不露的巨獸
書店以不起眼的門面對外經營
在重重書架後頭
它卻兀自生長
以一種初生星球的能量、暴力
和不可思議的可能性……

向晚時
我們總聽見近處、遠方

各種支架鬆動、潛行躡行的聲響
或土著在斷簡殘篇中搬桌動椅⋯⋯
對此我早已見怪不怪
我踮腳取下一本殷代出版的植物誌
水聲從架上空出的縫隙傳來
我專心翻閱
端坐如晷
渺小如蟻
然後換另一本書
好奇索讀
直到知識打烊⋯⋯

(1994)

Bookstore in a Dream

The forest that awes and fascinates us the most
is this bookstore.

In a district in decline
behind an address plate forever overlooked by the postman
hundreds of miles of bookshelves of all descriptions and
stone tiles, wood paneling, and
muddy corridors
congested, sprawling
stretch knowledge to
the reaches that electricity has not yet reached:
covered in cobwebs, in mystery miasma,
the foyers of mice and moths, sewers,
carpets knee-deep in water and
secret rooms with keys forever lost...

And bookshelves—tier upon tiers, hung with animal
    specimens,
ruined flags, family crests,
sealed windows, drawers with memory loss
displaying for us cavern after cavern
the savage face of human wisdom...

Nobody, not even the 89-year-old third-generation
    shopkeeper, Mr. L.,
Nobody knows the bookstore's true dimensions—

not even the literature professor Professor T., who last
        year in pursuit of some
        remaindered book,
was submerged forever in the quicksand of letters,
or the critic who, after many years, came dashing out of a
        mural
or the new breed of bats biting his neck...
Really, even in the closely guarded stacks east of Section
        B—
in the shrubbery, mainly of biographies and fables—
we will occasionally run into the
skeletons of the lost...

The maze that most amazes us
is this bookstore!

In an age filled with breathless change
we are close to tears singing the praises
of that immobile, insoluble, unrevealing iceberg
and to read—
to read of those rare, abstruse souls
and those indefatigable daydreams
is the ritual sacrifice of our youth...

Like a giant beast in hiding
through a quiet storefront is open for business

but past its ranges of bookshelves
it is still growing
with the energy, violence, and inconceivable possibilities
of a newborn star...

Toward evening
we always hear, far and near,
the woodwork coming loose and stealthy steps
or aborigines moving tables and chairs among scraps of
    ancient writing...
These strange things are no longer strange to me
On tiptoe I pick a botany book from the Yin dynasty
and the sound of water comes through the gap on the shelf
I focus on flipping pages
sitting straight as a sundial
tiny as an ant
then trade it for another book
Curiously scanning
until knowledge calls it a day...

(1994)

(Translated by Maghiel van Crevel)

地球之島

時光
當我回到地球　人類已離開許久
森林已收復了城市　鷗鳥還在河口逗留
無數棄置的錶心像貝殼遍布沙灘
有的積着海水　有的還在走動

進化
當我回到地球　人類已離開許久
夕陽頻頻回顧　成排貨棧空置的碼頭
海豚無辜的眼神隱約閃爍下一次文明的燧火
被野放的寵物隔代遺傳着不解的憂鬱與溫柔

對象
當我回到地球　文明已經打烊
除了還沒耗盡的燈火　夜晚已交還給月亮
雨林樹海的傘蓋下　一萬座城市已被安葬
夜行動物繁殖着更多窺視　在沒有崇高觀點的殿堂

聲音
當我回到地球　妳和他們都已遠離
我在無人的巨大球形島嶼獨行
聆聽這佔用太多空間的孤寂
空曠的宇宙像高八度的耳鳴

海洋

見過藍鯨那樣巨大的飛禽嗎？
海洋，只是太濃、太厚或太藍的大氣
有光就可以穿越，有鰓就可以飛翔
歌聲傳得好遠，永遠都不會沉澱

呼吸

海洋，只是太濃、太厚或太藍的大氣
這樣的想像讓我的想像比較容易呼吸
但別把天空從我們的體腔放走
否則海洋將侵入你的肺　把所有想像化為泡沫

滿月

我們久已不在沙灘生殖或產卵
但是滿月依然教我們小腹發脹
鯨魚和浮游生物水乳交融和善的獵食
至今我們體內仍遺傳着最初的海洋

裸體

最美滿的肉體，是被擁抱，被海水擁抱的裸體吧？
水溫是你唯一的衣縷
孤獨是你唯一的被褥
死亡是這麼的，這麼的平淡無奇

潮汐

不時有些深海的內臟被沖到沙灘上
曝曬成動物或植物的屍骸
這是這顆行星時刻進行的新陳代謝
46億歲的溫柔巨獸舔着全世界的海岸

Earth Island

Time

By the time I return to earth humankind has left long ago
Forests have re-conquered cities gulls still sport at the
   river mouth
Countless watch-faces are strewn on the shore like seashells
Some fogged up by seawater, some still running

Evolution

By the time I return to earth humankind has left long ago
The setting sun gives parting looks rows of gantries on an
   empty wharf
Innocent dolphin eyes flash the torchlight of the next
   civilization
Pets turned loose pass down pointless traits of tender
   melancholy

Mate

By the time I return to earth civilization has closed up shop
Except for lamps not yet burnt out night is given back to
   the moon
A myriad cities buried under the oceanic rainforest canopy
Beady nocturnal glances teem in shrines with no holy
   perspective

Sound

By the time I return to earth you and the rest have already
    left
I walk through this giant deserted spherical island
Straining my ears in a solitude that takes up too much space
the cosmic vastness like level 8 tinnitus

Ocean

Have you seen a flying creature as big as a blue whale?
The ocean is just atmosphere, too dense or too thick or
    too blue
Light can shine through it, fins can fly in it
Song carries far and never subsides

Breath

The ocean is just atmosphere. too dense or too thick or
    too blue
To imagine this lets my imagination breathe easier
But do not cast the sky from your body cavity
Or the ocean will invade your lungs change imagination
    into bubbles

Full Moon

It has been long since we mated and laid eggs on a beach
But the full moon still makes our abdomens swell
Blue whales and plankton strike the chord of benign foraging
The primordial sea is still passed down in bodies

Nudity

Isn't the loveliest flesh embraced in nakedness, embraced
    by the sea?
Water's temperature your only garment
Solitude your only quilted comforter
How very commonplace death can be

Ebb Tide

Sometimes the deep ocean's entrails wash ashore
Exposed to sun they turn into plant or animal remains
This is our planet's constant metabolism
A tender beast 4.6 billion years old licks the world's shore

(Translated by Denis Mair)

我

是的吾愛，在第一行之後
我就必須現身了
帶着「我」在古典時代的謙虛、隱遁
和此刻的急切、張揚
來向妳展現躲在「我」後面的我
在文字上可以被杜撰的
豐盛可能
以及它所暗示的
在現實上無須兌現的
豐盛可能

當然「我」仍將謹守文學內外的
真誠與矯飾
那是妳專心閱讀的基礎
也是和第一人稱若即若離的我
在愛戀與創作中
和「我」之間的
默契與承諾

但是「我」似乎不以為意
他繼續握着妳的手
以輕吐出來的甜言蜜語
彈奏着妳的睫毛
用精巧串連的
動人詞彙
陳述並承諾着

我即使在文學作品裏
也無法做到的事
我只有適時中斷此刻的書寫
深深吻住妳
讓「我」窒息

Me

Indeed, my love, after the very first line
I must show what I am truly made of
With the humble seclusion of a classical era "me"
And the flagrant urgency of this moment
Disclosing the "me" that is hidden behind me
Abundant possibilities
That can be concocted in writing
And the secret promise it carries
Abundant possibilities
That need never be cashed in for the real

Of course the "I" serves sincerity and artifice,
        inside and outside of literature
It provides the basis of your focused reading
And is the tacit accord and promise
In tender ties and creative work
Between "me" and the me
That is uneasily linked to the first person pronoun

But the "I" seems to take it all for granted
He continues to hold your hand
With gushing endearments
he plays a melody on your eyelashes
With touching vocabulary strung along
As deftly as beads
Expounding and promising

Things I cannot even accomplish
in works of literature
I have to break off this writing just in time
To give you a deep kiss
Before "I" can be stifled

(Translated by Denis Mair)

妳

「妳」永遠是最靠近我的
只要我有話想說
「妳」總是第一個知道
或第一個不知道
正如此刻
一個被濕冷的寒流所宵禁的夜晚
一張被疲憊盤據的電腦桌前
我尚未啟齒
而妳
已經在句中守望
不管知道或不知道

不論我要讓你知道或不知道
我總知道
妳總會
以妳所含糊象徵的
近處或遠處的幸福
注視着最憂鬱的那一行詩句
以妳的美麗與寂靜
梳理着我中年的感傷

雖然妳一直懷疑
文中的「妳」不全是妳
即使重點的描述符合
憑着女性的直覺

妳相信隱隱然有一些「妳」
並不是指妳

但，正如此刻，
我所極力傾訴
極力杜撰的
不一直都是妳嗎

只要妳
持續那無可比擬的
美麗與憂傷
持續在詩中聆聽
又持續在詩外讀我
妳永遠都是妳啊

You

You are forever closest to me
If only I have something to say
You will always be the first to know
Or the first not to know
Such as at this moment
as a damp cold-front imposes its curfew
In front of a computer desk entwined in weariness
Before my utterance begins
You keep watch for me
Within a sentence
Knowing or unknowing

Whether I let you know or not
I always know
You will always have a way
Of gazing at my poem's most melancholy line
With that near or distant happiness
You vaguely symbolize
Sorting through my middle-aged grief
With your beauty and your silence

Though you have suspicions
As to whether the written you is wholly "you"
Despite correspondence of salient features
via feminine intuition
You believe some *yous* do not refer to you

Yet even at this moment
Could what I confide with utmost feeling
And concoct with utmost wit
be anything but you?

If only you keep up
This beauty and sadness
No one else can touch
Keep up this listening within poems
Keep reading me outside of poems
You will always be you

(Translated by Denis Mair)

1955年生於臺北。臺灣大學哲學系畢業，美國威斯康辛大學東亞所碩士、博士班肄業。曾任報社副總編輯、電台台長、雜誌及出版社發行人，也擔任過臺北市政府新聞處處長、香港光華中心主任，並任教於大學中文系。
作品以詩、散文和遊記為主；風格強烈，知性、感性兼具，以精確、細膩的語法著稱，以觀察力和想像力見長，對新一代詩人有極大的影響力。主要出版作品有：詩集《畫冊》、《光之書》、《傾斜之書》、《擲地無聲書》、《寶寶之書》、《黑色鑲金》、《夢中書房》、《夢中邊陲》、《地球之島》，散文集《M湖書簡》、《亞熱帶習作》、《泥炭紀》等。

Born in Taipei, Lo Chih Cheng (Luo Zhicheng) graduated from the Department of Philosophy of National Taiwan University. After having worked as editor for the *China Times* for two years, he went to study at University of Wisconsin, Madison, where he earned an MA in East Asian Languages and Literature and completed course work in the doctoral program. Since returning to Taiwan, he has assumed various editorial positions at newspapers, magazines and publishing companies and became the publisher of several publishing companies and has taught at several universities for more than twenty years. Active in the media, including television and broadcasting, he also served some official positions such as Commissioner of the Department of Information of Taipei city government and Director of Kwang Hua Information and Cultural Center (Hong Kong). Lo published his first book of poems, which he not only self-financed but also designed and illustrated, in 1975. Since then he has published more than ten books of poetry, five books of prose or critical essays, two books of travel writing and various translations. Lo has received several important literary prizes, organized the 2002, 2003 and 2010 Taipei Poetry Festivals and participated in the 2004 French Spring Poetry Festival at Paris and the 2005 Literary Festival at Berlin. Lo's literary works are famous for their philosophical profoundness, imaginative imagery, lyrical syntax and original insight. Already an established poet in the 1970s, he has continued to influence poets of a younger generation.

出版 Publisher
香港中文大學出版社 The Chinese University Press

封面及平面設計 Cover and Graphic Designer
朱德華 Almond Chu

製稿及分色 Art Work and Colour Separation
明星鐳射分色有限公司 Star Laser Graphic Co. Ltd.

印刷 Printer
宏亞印務有限公司 Asia One Printing Ltd.

出版日期 Date of Publication
二零一一年十月 October 2011

國際書號 ISBN
978-962-996-525-9

香港國際詩歌之夜2011主辦單位
International Poetry Nights in Hong Kong 2011 Organizers

香港中文大學東亞研究中心
Centre for East Asian Studies, The Chinese University of Hong Kong

香港城市大學人文社會科學院
College of Liberal Arts and Social Sciences, City University of Hong Kong

香港科技大學人文社會科學學院
School of Humanities and Social Science,
The Hong Kong University of Science and Technology

香港國際詩歌之夜2011協辦單位
International Poetry Nights in Hong Kong 2011 Co-organizer
木刻文化出版有限公司 MUKE Publishing Limited